By Their House

Dona Herweck Rice

Publishing Credits

Rachelle Cracchiolo, M.S.Ed., *Publisher*
Conni Medina, M.A.Ed., *Managing Editor*
Nika Fabienke, Ed.D., *Content Director*
Véronique Bos, *Creative Director*
Shaun N. Bernadou, *Art Director*
Carol Huey-Gatewood, M.A.Ed., *Editor*
John Leach, *Assistant Editor*
Courtney Roberson, *Senior Graphic Designer*

Image Credits: p.10 (top) f8grapher/iStock; all other images from iStock and/or Shutterstock.

Teacher Created Materials
5301 Oceanus Drive
Huntington Beach, CA 92649-1030
www.tcmpub.com

ISBN 978-1-4938-9851-0

Printed in China
Nordica.082018.CA21800936

Look at the many 

by their  .

Look at the many 

flowers

by their  .

house

Look at the many 

ants

by their  .

house

Look at the many 

birds

by their  .

house

Look at the many 
dogs

by their  .
house

Look at the many 

cats

by their  .

house

Look at the many 

logs

by their  .

house

Look at the many 

rocks

by their  .

house

Look at the many 

cars

by their  .

house

Look at the many  people

by their  house .

High-Frequency Words

New Words

by
look
many
their

Review Words

at
the